READER'S DELIGHT

Biography

of

Lok Nayak
Jai Prakash Narayan

Revolutionary & Freedom Fighter

READER'S DELIGHT

An Imprint of Ramesh Publishing House

NEW DELHI

Published by: Alok Kumar Gupta for Reader's Delight
(An Imprint of Ramesh Publishing House)

Admin. Office:

12-H, New Daryaganj Road, Opp. Officers' Mess,
New Delhi-110002 ① 23261567, 23275224, 23275124
E-mail: info@rameshpublishinghouse.com
Website: www.rameshpublishinghouse.com

Showroom:

- Balaji Market, New Delhi-6 ① 23253720, 23282525
- 4457, Nai Sarak, Delhi-6, ① 23918938

INDEMNIFICATION CLAUSE

- This book is being sold/distributed on the condition and understanding that the information given herein are merely for guidance and reference and must not be taken as authority, and neither the author nor the publishers individually or collectively, shall be responsible to indemnify the buyer/user/possessor of this book beyond the selling price of this book for any reason under any circumstances. If you do not agree to it, please do not buy/accept/use/possess this book.

- Though every care has been taken in printing this book, errors or ommissions might have crept inadvertently. The publishers shall be obliged if such error or ommission is brought to their notice.

- Subject to Delhi jurisdiction.

Book Code: A-106

ISBN: 978-93-86298-91-1

Preface

The Biography of Lok Nayak Jai Prakash Narayan is the brief life sketch of a great revolutionary and freedom fighter who not only worked with Mahatma Gandhi and Jawaharlal Nehru to win the freedom of India but also worked with the great revolutionaries and socialists like Dr. Ram Manohar Lohia.

JP was a staunch Marxist but joined the freedom movement with Indian National Congress on the invitation of Jawaharlal Nehru. He was also engaged in many revolutionary activities and even raised the 'Freedom Brigade'. He was arrested many times and spent many years of his life in various jails of India.

He differed with the Congress on the matter of Partition of India and ultimately parted ways with the Congress to form the Praja Socialist Party. Later, he left active politics and joined the 'Bhoodan Movement' of Acharya Vinoba Bhave and Sarvodaya work.

In the late 60's and 70's he was again active in mass movements in Gujarat and Bihar. He was again arrested during the 'Emergency' promulgated by Indira Gandhi.

The inside pages consist of an inspiring account of his life—how a humble village boy of Bihar rose to become a 'Lok Nayak' or 'The People's Hero' of India.

—Publisher

Contents

Introduction

My interest is not in the caputre of power,
but in the control of power by the people.

Jai Prakash Narayan was an Indian independence activist and political leader. Popularly referred to as JP or Lok Nayak (The People's Hero), he actively participated in the civil disobedience movement against British rule in India.

JP returned to India after higher studies at US in 1929. Impressed by his ideals, Jawaharlal Nehru invited him

Jai Prakash Narayan

to join the Indian National Congress which he accepted. Mahatma Gandhi was also impressed by him.

JP became very active in the surging Indian independence movement. He participated in the civil disobedience against

British rule and was arrested and imprisoned in 1932. During his imprisonment he met Ram Manohar Lohia and other national leaders, which strengthened his nationalist fervour. After his release, he played a major role in the founding of the Congress Socialist Party, a left-wing group within the Congress Party, and was made its General Secretary.

JP intensified his role in the Indian freedom struggle and was imprisoned by the British again in 1939 for his opposition to Indian participation in World War II on the side of Britain. But he made good his escape in a dramatic way.

In 1942, Mahatma Gandhi launched the Quit India Movement. During this time JP planned to start an underground movement for freedom. However he was recaptured by the British in 1943.

JP was finally released in 1946. By this time he had grown so passionate about the freedom struggle that he tried to persuade the Congress leaders to adopt a more violent approach against the British.

India eventually gained independence in 1947. Along with several other socialists, he left the Congress Party in 1948. A few years later he played a major role in forming the Praja Socialist Party in 1952.

Before long JP became tired of the party politics and decided to dedicate his life to the Bhoodan Movement, founded by Vinoba Bhave. However, his interest in politics was re-ignited in the late 1950s and once again he became active in political activities.

JP gained much prominence as a politician in the late 1960s. In 1965 he was presented with the Ramon Magsaysay Award for public service. After the nation suffered high inflation and unemployment among other problems in 1974, the Nav Nirman Andolan movement of Gujarat asked him to lead a peaceful agitation.

In his seventies at the time, he led a silent procession at Patna. The procession was lathi-charged but nothing could deter the patriot's spirit. He addressed a large crowd at Gandhi Maidan on 5 June, 1974 which was initiated by students in protest against the corruption in the government of Bihar. Also called Total Revolution Movement and JP Movement, it later turned against Prime Minister Indira Gandhi's government at the Centre and became a satyagraha of sorts.

JP suffered from kidney failure, diabetes and heart ailments during his later years and died on 8 October, 1979. He was posthumously honoured with the Bharat Ratna, India's highest civilian award, in 1999 in recognition of his social work.

Jai Prakash Narayan Museum, Arcohm Lucknow

Early Life and Education

*True politics is about promotion
of human happiness.*

Jai Prakash Narayan was born on October 11, 1902 in a village namely Sitab-diara in Saran district of Bihar. Sitab-diara village lies some eight kilometers from Patna. He was the son of Harsh Dayal, a middle-class, minor government official and Phulrani Devi. He was the fourth child of his parents. He had two brothers and three sisters.

After finishing primary education, Jai Prakash went to Patna for his High School education. The nationalist movement was very strong in Bihar those days. In 1917, Mahatma Gandhi had gone to Bihar to investigate the condition of labour in Indigo plantations. By using the non-violent technique of Satyagraha against the British plantation owners successfully, he had attracted the attention of all the nationalists to the novel method of non-violent resistance to injustice.

Jai Prakash was also duly impressed. He started reading Gandhiji's articles in 'Young India'. He discarded the western style of dress, and took to wearing coarse Khadi clothes. But still his attraction towards revolutionaries from Bengal went on increasing.

In 1919, he passed his Matriculation in first class and earned a 'merit scholarship'. He enrolled his name in the Science College in Patna. His ambition was to be a scientist and serve his motherland.

Jai Prakash lived an eventful life. Those days, Bal Gangadhar Tilak, the leader of the 'Garam Dal' of the Indian National Congress gave the slogan 'Swaraj is my Birth Right and I shall have it'. The historical Russian Revolution also took place in the year 1917.

All these events had a tremendous impact on Jai Prakash. He read about Gandhiji's life writings and the Bhagawad Geeta. The simplicity of Gandhiji and his identification with the common man had a profound impact on him. But Gopal Krishna Gokhale was first to influence him. Jai Prakash even wrote a tearful poem when Gokhale died.

❑❑❑

Marriage & Movement

> *If you really care for freedom, liberty.*
> *There cannot be any democracy or*
> *liberal institution without politics.*

In 1920, Jai Prakash was married to Prabhavati Devi, the eldest daughter of a rich and influential resident of Patna, Babu Braj Kishore Prasad. He was the well-known Congress leader of Bihar. Jai Prakash had then completed the eighteenth year of his age while Prabhavati Devi was an innocent girl of only fourteen.

It was the second year of his marriage and his Intermediate examination was only a few days away when Gandhiji started his non-cooperation movement.

Jai Prakash got the opportunity in 1920 to listen

Jai Prakash Narayan with Prabhavati Devi

to the speeches of both Maulana Azad and Jawaharlal Nehru in Patna. Gandhiji called upon advocates and students to boycott courts and colleges respectively, Deshbandhu C.R. Das and Pandit Motilal Nehru had already given up their practices. In Patna, Maulana Mazrul Haq and Dr. Rajendra Prasad had followed their example.

Jai Prakash Narayan, in his speeches proudly refers to these events in his early life, while calling upon college students in Bihar to give up their studies for a year and throw themselves whole heartedly in the movement for a total revolution.

He wrote : "As a boy, like most boys of those days, I was an ardent nationalist and learned towards the revolutionaries cult of which Bengal was the noble leader at that time. But even then the story of the South African Satyagraha had fascinated my young heart. Before my revolutionary learnings could mature, Gandhiji's first non-cooperation movement swept over the land as a strangely up-lifting hurricane.

But all of a sudden, Mahatma Gandhi abandoned his plan of Satyagraha in February 1922, as a violent mob at Chaurichaura burnt down a police station and killed several policemen. Gandhiji undertook a 5-day fast of atonement for the tragedy and withdrew the campaign of non-cooperation movement.

❏ ❏ ❏

Higher Education

> *A violent revolution has always brought*
> *forth a dictatorship of some kind or the other... .*
> *After a revolution, a new privileged class of rulers*
> *and exploiters grows up in the course of time to*
> *which the people at large is once again subject.*

Jai Prakash Narayan decided to continue his studies further. He enrolled himself as a student in Bihar Vidyapeeth, an institution founded by the nationalist leaders. He passed his Intermediate examination with merit.

Jai Prakash Narayan wanted to join higher studies. But there was no teaching facility of science beyond Intermediate in the Vidyapeeth. He did not like to join the English Government Aided Educational Institutions. So, he decided to go to USA for higher education.

Jai Prakash confided to his wife, his future plans and told her of his intention to go to America. She readily gave her consent. Jai Prakash left Patna with a heavy heart.

His wife evolved to become a prominent freedom fighter and Gandhian in her own right. Prabhavati moved to Gandhi's ashram when JP went to the US for his higher studies.

On the 16th of August 1922, he sailed for the United States via Rangoon, Hong Kong and Yakohama in Japan. He landed in California in the second week of October 1922. He had very little money with him.

He did several odd jobs to pay for his education there and these experiences made him aware about the difficulties faced by the working class.

On enquiries, he came to know that the new semester at the University of California at Berkeley was to start in January 1923. So he decided to work, earn his living and save a few dollars for paying his fees. With the help of one, Sher Khan a pathan foreman, he found a job as an agricultural labourer on a big farm.

Surprisingly as it may seem, young Jai Prakash worked for ten hours a day with only an hour's recess in between for lunch. At the rate of 40 cents an hour, he used to earn about four dollars a day. Within a few weeks, he earned enough money for paying his fees. He thus enrolled himself for the second year in Science at the California University.

His struggles to make ends meet in a foreign land made him realize the difficulties faced by the working class. After being introduced to Karl Marx's 'Das Kapital', JP became convinced that Marxism was the way to alleviate the suffering of the masses.

Earning while Learning

Power comes invariably to be usurped by a handful of the most ruthless among the erstwhile revolutionaries when power comes out of the barrel of a gun and the gun is not in the hands of the common people.

All this experience of "earning while learning" brought Jai Prakash in close contact with farm labourers in a country which was fabulously rich. For Jai Prakash who was bent upon securing a degree of an American University, physical labour had become a sheer necessity.

But at Berkeley, another difficulty arose. An increase in the amount of fees for the next semester was announced by the University authorities. Jai Prakash had to leave the California University and again go to a farm for making a saving for future. He then went to Iowa and joined the University there. He stayed there for one year. Jai Prakash and five of his Indian friends used to cook their own food together and share the expenses. He used to earn money on Sundays and holidays by taking odd jobs and even household chores. It was in Iowa University itself that Jai

Prakash came to be called and known as JP, a nick name formed from his initials which has stuck to him since.

Even thereafter, Jai Prakash had to go from place to place in search of suitable work and had to leave one University to join another. He left Iowa and went to Chicago, where he stayed for two and a half year. Then he went to Wisconsin and also to Ohio.

It is surprising to learn that during this period Jai Prakash had to work as a waiter and even as a scavenger in hotels, cleaning toilets, as a shoe shiner and as an assistant in the barber's shop. Many a time he had also worked as a casual labourer, undertaking to shovel off accumulated snow from the doors and gates of American house-owners. His readiness to do any kind of work showed how deep and strong was his urge for learning.

Jai Prakash Narayan who originally was a vegetarian, had taken to non-vegetarian in the difficult and changed circumstances that he had to face in a foreign country, in a foreign culture. Once however, he was required to work in a factory where beef and mutton were being dressed up and packed for despatch. He was so shocked and overwhelmed by nausea at the sight of the huge mass of red raw flesh inside the factory that for a few weeks he could not eat non-vegetarian food. He also asked for change of work and got a job in the electric power house of the same factory.

❑❑❑

Introduction to Marxism

*It (Communism) did not offer an answer
to the question : Why should a man be good?*

At the various American Universities Jai Prakash studied Natural Science, Economics and Sociology. He came into contact with American, Russian, Polish, German and French students. He had struck deep friendship with some of them. He was also drawn to some kindly professors.

One Jew, Abraham Landy-by name, who was both a post-graduate student and lecturer at the Wisconsin University, was a communist by conviction. As a card-holding member of the Communist Party of America, he used to run a secret cell at the university campus. Jai Prakash came under the influence of this friend of his and started attending the secret meetings at the cell and reading communist literature. Landy introduced Jai Prakash to Marxism. Under his and Manuel Gomez's, a Mexican born leader of the American Communist Party influence, Jai Prakash studied Marx, Engels, Lenin and Trotsky.

As a Marxist, Jai Prakash Narayan also believed that 'political freedom must be accompanied with freedom from economic exploitation and poverty.

JP wanted to go to Russia from USA but he had to give up his desire to visit the land of the first Communist revolution in the world. He later continued his studies at the Ohio University and took BA Degree in Sociology. He got a scholarship also and while continuing as a post-graduate student of Sociology, he started teaching some lower classes.

He passed his MA and was about to enrol himself as a student for PhD, when a letter from his home informed him that his mother was seriously ill. With the help of a Maharashtrian friend and with the money sent to him by his father, he returned to India in September 1929, via England, France, Italy, Port Said and Colombo. And he reached his home village Sitab-diara, his mother bathed him in tears of unsullied joy.

JP's sojourn in the USA for full seven years in quest of knowledge was indeed a saga of patience, perseverance, hardships and hardwork. When he had set foot on the soil of the American continent in 1922, he was a callow youth of only twenty years of age, fresh from his feudal surroundings in Bihar, when he returned to India in 1929, he was a well experienced, wise young man. His father had then retired from service. His wife, Prabhavati was staying with Gandhiji at Sabarmati Ashram and had taken the vow of celibacy. JP respected the decision of his wife. ❑❑❑

Meeting JL Nehru

Democracy cannot be made secure and strong without peace. Peace and democracy are the two sides of a coin. Neither of them can survive without the other.

At the time that Jai Prakash returned from America, nationalist feeling had reached a peak of frenzy. Early in 1930 Mahatma Gandhi launched the Salt Satyagraha. Jai Prakash joined the fray with whole-hearted enthusiasm.

Jawaharlal Nehru and Jai Prakash Narayan

A few days after Jai Prakash's return, a session of the Bihar provincial congress was held at Munger. Rajendra Prasad presided over the meetings, and Sardar Patel too was present. The victory at Bardoli had raised their spirits and given the session an added importance. The chief issue at Munger session was whether the nationalist movement should demand full independence, or whether a promise of dominion status was enough.

The congressmen were all for the more radical demand, complete independence. The older leaders opposed them. Jai Prakash was at that session as an observer. From Sitab-diara he went with Prabhavati to Wardha to meet Bapu. Prabhavati went because she wanted to return to her duties at the ashram. After the working-committee deliberations, Jai Prakash and Jawaharlal Nehru were introduced to each other.

From Wardha, Jai Prakash and Prabhavati accompained Gandhiji to Lahore, where Jawaharlal presided over the Congress session. Thousands of people marched in tumultuous processions. Great shouts of "Inquilab Zindabad" (Long live the revolution) rant the air. This was the session at which Nehru announced that Congress would fight for complete independence (Poorna Swaraj).

The meetings were drawing to a close. The big question was, what will Prabha do now? Would she go with Bapu to Wardha or choose to stay with her husband? Neither husband nor wife seemed to want to broach this ticklish subject. Prabha went to look for Bapu to seek his advice. Bapu said: "It is your Dharma, your duty. You must go with your husband". She bent down to touch Bapu's feet and burst into tears.

One day Jawaharlal Nehru came up to Jai Prakash and asked him what he was doing. Jai Prakash answered that he wanted to work for the country and join the Congress. "In that case, come to Allahabad" said Jawaharlal. As Congress President, Jawaharlal wanted to appoint Jai Prakash a

Secretary in the Labour Department of the Congress. Jai Prakash agreed to go to Allahabad and join.

It was the beginning of 1930, Jai Prakash was in Allahabad and Prabha with him. They rented a house in the George town locality in Allahabad for sixty rupees. Their total income was a hundred and fifty rupees a month. Nehru said "Why are you unnecessarily spending so much money in the rent? Why don't you come and stay at Swaraj Bhavan? So that was there Jai Prakash and Prabha moved next. Nehru became more and more impressed with Jai Prakash's acute intelligence.

Soon after the movement of 1930 began. But at about the same time, his mother fell ill, and Jai Prakash returned to his home. His mother died at the end of this illness, and Jai Prakash was unable to involve himself with the movement any more. He stayed on in the village for a while. Financially the family was in necessity straits, and Jai Prakash had no thought of leaving them to secure for themselves. Kamala Nehru, wife of Jawaharlal Nehru, wrote Prabha a letter that Jai Prakashji should come back and attend to his work.

❏ ❏ ❏

Freedom Struggle

Only those who have no faith or confidence in the people or are unable to win the people's confidence take to violent means.

The Congress celebrated, "Independence day" all over India on 26th January 1930. Mahatma Gandhi, authorised by the Congress commended the Civil Disobedience movement in March by starting the Salt Satyagraha and the march to Dandi. The whole country was inflamed.

Jai Prakash and Prabha were quickly down into the centre of the agitation and went to Allahabad. Mahatma Gandhi was detained in May that year. The Congress was banned, but its meetings continued and its public support grew, and leaflets and directives issued by it continued to find their way to all parts of the country.

Jai Prakash Narayan

It was the first time in the history of Britsh rule that the government was humbled. Lord Irwin summoned Gandhi for talks in February 1931. The Satyagraha was called off. The ban on Congress was lifted. Mahatma Gandhi left for Round Table Conference in London. The Viceroy agreed to release the civil disobedience prisoners and to allow people living on the coast to manufacture salt.

During this period, Jai Prakash recieved the news that his father had a paralytic stroke. There was no option for him but to take leave or absence from his work. The family was in grave financial trouble. Now there was no money to take care of the father's medical bill. Jai Prakash wrote to Gandhi and described his predicament. Bapu replied to say that Jai Prakash's primary loyality was undoubtedly towards his father and family and that he must rush to their aid. He also wrote to GD Birla asking him if he could somehow help Jai Prakash, suggesting that a teaching post at Pilani college would do fine. The government however would not have permitted a political firebrand like Jai Prakash to teach at Pilani, and so Birla offered Jai Prakash a job as his secretary.

Jai Prakash Narayan stayed with Birla for six months until the Gandhi-Irwin pact was signed. Immediately after Jawaharlal Nehru summoned Jai Prakash to return to work for the new legal Congress.

A winter morning in 1940, Jai Prakash had been served with a warrant of arrest. He had been charged with making an unlawful speech on the 18th of February that year at

Jamshedpur. Two days later, Jai Prakash was put behind bars in the Chaivasa jail. Gandhi and Nehru protested against this flagrant repressive measure. Gandhi wrote: "The arrest of Jai Prakash Narayan is unfortunate. He is no ordinary worker. He is an authority on Socialism. He has forsaken all for the sake of the deliverance of his country. His industry is tireless".

Nine months later, Jai Prakash was removed from Chaivasa to the Hazaribagh jail, where he joined the political detenus of the communist party and the forward block. Instead of comradeship he was treated with hostility.

In the jail, Jai Prakash's political work continued uninterrupted. To those who were willing to listen, he talked endlessly about politics and political economy. Gradually, he established contact with associates whose activities had not been curtailed by imprisonment. Soon, by smuggling out despatches, he somehow managed to write articles, they were signed—simply 'a Congress Socialist'.

After a few months Jai Prakash Narayan was released and he resolved not to allow himself to be imprisoned again. This meant living and working in hiding, with the utmost secrecy. It did not mean abandoning his political mission or curtailing his activity.

Immediately after he contacted Gandhi and then Subhash Chandra Bose, still intent on bringing about a rapproachement between the two, but his talks with Bose were unfruitful. From Calcutta, Jai Prakash went to Bihar to bolster the Peasant movement (led by Swamy Sahajananda) in its struggle against the repressive machinery of the state.

From Bihar he travelled to Gujarat and then to Bombay, where he attended meetings and met other leaders. And then suddenly he was rearrested and sent to the Arthur Road Jail in Bombay city. And from there, to Deoli camp, where he joined about 500 prisoners under political detention. Once again Jai Prakash utilised this period of enforced 'rest' in busying himself in the only kind of political activity open to him.

By 1942, the war had moved to India's doorstep. In February that year Singapore fell to the Japanese, and Rangoon a month later. Churchill and Roosevelt turned their attention to the Eastern Theatre of war. The prisoners were released soon after the bombing of Pearl Harbour. Now, the fall of Rangoon prompted Churchill to despatch to India in March 1942, a British Cabinet Minister, Sir Stafford Cripps. The Indian political deadlock had suddenly become a matter of grave concern not only to the British, but to their allies, the USA and China, and they pressed for a solution to the Internal Conflict.

The Cripps Mission had aroused hopes in the Congress circles and suspicion among the Muslim leagues, but turned out to be disappointing to the former and stimulating to the latter. The failure of the Mission further sharpened the Congress hostility towards the British. The approach of Japan to India's Eastern frontier aroused among the Congressmen mixed feelings of hope and fear.

There was the fear that Japan might turn out to be a new Imperialist, Nehru's anti-British attitude was not, therefore a plea to submit to Japan. The Congress now looked for guidance of Gandhi, who was in a more uncompromising mood than ever. He decided that British must 'Quit India' immediately.

Immediately after the Congress Working Committee passed a resolution on the 6th July 1942 asking the British to withdraw from India, threatening a civil disobedience movement if they remained. The revolution was endorsed by the All India Congress Committee on the 8th August 1942 in Bombay. The very next day all members of the Congress Working Committee and Mahatma Gandhi were arrested and the Indian National Congress was outlawed. Gandhi reiterated his call for non-violent agitation, but his mood had changed and it was not clear that he would condemn the nation for choosing whatever method it found suitable to force the British to quit. Gandhi had sounded the clarion call 'Do or Die'.

Hundreds of thousands of people responded to Gandhi's call passionately. Finding no Congress leaders outside prison to guide them, they resorted to violence. Trains were derailed and looted, police stations were set ablaze and telegraph lines cut. Particularly in Bihar and UP the apparatus of the British government was ground to a complete halt, and the army was called in.

With all the Congress leaders behind bars, the socialist assumed the task of master-minding the movement and directing the rampaging crowds. Everyday there were reports of police firings and fresh arrests. Achyut Patwardhan, Dr. Lohia and their companions formed a central mobilisation committee. At the best of times, however, they were little-known substitutes for the Congress stalwarts.

All this time, Jai Prakash Narayan was pacing his cell in rage of frustration. At the high-tide of the movement, he found himself chained and confined unable to play any role at all. He decided to attempt a jail-break and explained his plans to the other inmates. The very next day the guards were changed and the security arrangements were intensified. Somehow the plan had leaked to the authorities, and it now seemed a more difficult project than ever.

Jai Prakash Narayan

August and September 1942 came and went. Many prisoners were tried, sentenced and despatched to jails in other parts of the country. As the number of prisoners in the jail dwindled, the armed guards were removed.

Jail Break

War leads us into more wars, and then into complete destruction. This alternative of nonviolence is the only answer to the situation the world is facing today.

The prisoners in the cells received a daily food ration worth 62 paise. Jai Prakash Narayan together with a group of Satyagrahis, protested against the treatment meted out to the prisoners. On the inferior diet which was entitled, Jai Prakash's health declined steadily, and his legs were afflicted with sciatica. Through all these difficulties, the plan of escape from prison kept turning over in his mind.

On Diwali morning, the inmates set about preparing for the festival. Sweets were prepared and the inmates sang bhajans. As evening approached, 42 diyas were lit to commemorate the events of that year, and the inmates toured the wards in procession singing and cheering with the festivals in full swing, JP and five other men slipped away under the cover of darkness and scaled the wall with the help of dhotis knotted together as a rope.

Their absence was not detected until the next morning. Those of the inmates who were in the know dropped the mosquito-nets over the beds of the six escapees and pretended as if they were unwell.

Early in the morning however the prison sirens began wailing and the prisoners awoke in a flurry to the news that the men had gone.

Jai Prakash Narayan left for Benares and landed at Nagraghat near the University. The Government announced a reward of ₹ 5000/- for his capture.

Jai Prakash Narayan quickly established contact with the men who were at the helm of affairs during the August movement in Northern India. Viswanath Misra, Sriram Sharma, Mohanlal Gautam; Benares was the storm centre of the movement in this part of the country.

A brief look around him to get acquainted with recent developments convinced him that Benares was not the place to be in. Wearing European clothes, and sporting a beard, Jai Prakash left for Bombay.

Here he found that his friends and associates were already working tirelessly to give the movement shape and coherence. Achyut Patvardhan, Jugal Kishore, Dr. Keskar, Diwakar, Aruna Asaf Ali, Sucheta Kripalani, Yusuf Meherally and many others had filled in positions of leadership vacated by the imprisioned Congress leaders.

The British unleashed a brutal repression to quell the movement. Everything had to be organised in secrecy. Emissaries were despatched all over the country to coordinate the activities of Nationalist bodies. The Congress and CSP periodicals and bulletins, which were banned, continued to appear from hidden hand presses and were circulated widely.

Jai Prakash Narayan jumped into the fray. After studying the situation, he penned in January 1943 the first of his historic letters: 'to all fighters for freedom'.

As Jai Prakash Narayan emerged at the forefront of the political struggle, the government intensified its efforts to recapture him.

To a political movement that had been shorn-of its most eminent leaders Jai Prakash Narayan's escape was a tonic. Now once again, there was confidence that the energies of the people would not be expanded in spontaneous random acts, but would be guided towards a clear objective.

Six months after his jail-break, Jai Prakash wrote the second of his letters entitled 'To all fighters for freedom', it appeared on the 1st September 1943:

"Every fighter for freedom is free to choose his own method. Those who believe in similar method should work together as a disciplined group...Where 'Do or Die' is the mantra of action, there is no room for recrimination whatever those who believe in non-violence may harbour the fear that those who practise violence may compromise the position of Gandhiji. That fear is unfounded. Gandhi's adherence to non-violence is so complete, his position in respect to it so clear, that not a hundred thousand Churchills and Anerys will be able to compromise him."

Jai Prakash Narayan's political involvement had never before been so hectic. Ever so often he went out on hurricane tours of the country, heavily disguised, constantly on the move so that no single indiscretion could catch up with him. It was also a time of great responsibility, and Jai Prakash rose to the occasion with great strength of purpose. He wrote a spate of articles and pamphlets, carefully analysing himself the rapidly unfolding political situation, and addressing himself to every section of the people. His writings were simple, cogent and clearcut, his own experience allowed to identify with certain sections of people, and his relentless logic adopted their point of view.

With the six escapees remaining at large, the Government announced that it had doubled the reward for their capture. Jai Prakash now had a reward of ₹ 10,000/- on his head, yet his political work continued unabated.

Raising Freedom Brigade

Those people who still believe that power and party-politics will be able to do some good are only sucking dry bones. This kind of politics is disintegrating and will countinue to do so till one day the disintegration is complete.

Jai Prakash Narayan attended an important meeting of the Central Co-ordinating Council of the movement at Delhi. At that meeting the plan of raising a freedom brigade was mooted and approved. Sucheta Kripalani, on behalf of the Gandhians, expressed her dismay; but her dissent was brushed aside. Further, the basis was laid for recruiting volunteers from among workers, peasants and students. Special attention had to be paid to the working class. Better methods of communication by Radio and Press would have to be devised and operated in secret. Jai Prakash Narayan assumed the task of raising a guerilla brigade, of educating it and preparing it for the struggle. Soon after these aims were agreed upon, he made preparations to leave for Nepal.

In the first flush of the August 1942 uprising small pockets of land had been liberated from the British and Panchayati Raj had been proclaimed. For a very short period these areas remained outside government control but nothing was done to consolidate these victories. A few police stations were looted, arms were seized, but as it became clear that the uprising in the rest of the country would not take place, Panchayati Raj came to an end.

It was clear to Jai Prakash Narayan that spontaneous armed uprising was not enough. His task in Nepal was to raise and train a freedom brigade of single-minded disciplined force. Initially it would be a small band of men, supplementing their resources through guerilla raids and surprise forays into India. Gradually, however as they grew in experience and support, the force would grow until it came to represent the militant nationalism of the Indian people. The resistance groups operating behind German lines in France and Poland furnished an operational blueprint of how the freedom brigade would work.

The guerilla squads were thus given a clear mission of destruction which would paralyse the machinery of the British Government. These systems were singled out for destruction :

1. Disruption of Communication lines including Telegraph, Telephone, Mail and Wireless lines, Railways, Roads, Bridges and Motor Vehicles of the enemy.

2. Disruption of Industrial Plants, Factories, Mills and Airports.

3. Incendiary activity, which covered destruction of Government documents, Buildings, Petrol Pumps, Arms and Ammunition by fire.

Guerilla units would suffice for most of these tasks, but Industrial sabotage would require special people 'planted' among the permanent work force who could undertake their tasks without attracting attention.

The Freedom Brigade, as envisaged, was to be more effective than individual terrorist action. In the first hand book, a special appeal was made to students and young revolutionaries to join the Brigade. Dr. Ram Manohar Lohia congratulated this revolution in the newspaper.

On the low-lying land near the river Kosi in Nepal, Jai Prakash lived in a thatched hut at a place called Bakro-Ka-Tapu. The blue print of the brigade had been widely circulated and it elicited a good response. Youths from Bihar, Bengal and the Eastern regions who had hitherto led an underground existence as terrorists began to arrive at this spot. More huts were constructed for them to live in. The organisation started off with two horses and a bullock-cart for its transport. Two dak runners were engaged to carry messages. The camp was situated at the base of a hill, which was selected as the site of a Radio Transmitter, and the first broadcasts carrying news of the revolution went on the air.

The first task force to be organised was the Bihar Freedom Brigade. Suraj Narayan assumed the responsibility as coordinator of the project. The whole province was scoured to find volunteers, and immediately afterwards, training camps were started. The first camp aimed at grooming an officer cadre for the Brigade, men who would eventually be able to lead independent columns of guerillas. Among this first group was Nityanand, who was killed by police at Sonebarsa in Bhagalpur some time later.

Jai Prakash Narayan had been at the camp for two months. The trailing of a revolutionary cadre and the propaganda work by the radio were regressing smoothly. But about this time, the British Government found out that Jai Prakash and Dr. Lohia were in Nepal. It soon became known that the Government was pressurising the Nepalese Government to arrest all the people involved in the venture. The camp began teeming with British spies and intelligence agents. Any moment an armed attack was expected.

Jai Prakash Narayan and the others began to make frenzied preparations to abandon the site and move up into the mountains. Jai Prakash went ahead to help raise some funds. The same day Shyam Nandan was arrested by a Nepalese armed unit. Jai Prakash, Dr. Lohia and two others were arrested a shortwhile later, and they were taken across the Kosi towards Hanuman Nagar for interrogation.

This was in May 1944, in Hanuman Nagar, they were interrogated by a Nepalese Magistrate. It was clear that his orders had come from the Government at Kathmandu, for repeatedly, he left the room to talk rapidly in Nepali on the Telephone. The British intelligence had supplied him with photographs of the ring leaders, and every now and again he peered anxiously into the prisoners faces.

Jai Prakash Narayan and the others stuck doggedly to their story that they were Bihari peasants fleeing from the injustice of British courts in India. Miraculously, the Magistrate did not recognise the men from the photographs, and he was convinced that Jai Prakash was not among them.

At midnight, two men stole into the vicinity of the court house and tried to find out where the men were kept captive. A sentry was overpowered, but his cry had alerted other guards, and very soon the rescue force was fighting its way to the guard room through a vicious cross-fire. It was a dark night and the whole building had been plunged in utter darkness when the lights were hit by gun fire. Taken by surprise and thrown into utter confusion, the Nepalese sentries preferred to leave the area and alert the authorities. Meanwhile the prisoners were set free from the guard room.

In rushing out Lohia and Jai Prakash had run into a bramble bush and hurt their feet. Their escape was thus slow, but by evening of the next day, they had re-crossed the Kosi and took shelter in an Ahir's house in the evening.

The next day they moved on again, skirting police outposts, sticking to the woods, then at Radhopur they hired a bullock-cart and headed in the direction of Bengal. The following day, the men broke up, and boarded separate trains for Calcutta.

The countrywide search by the Government for Jai Prakash Narayan was not relaxed, whenever it was suspected that he might be hiding, the police raided shops, houses and hotels.

❑❑❑

Arrested Again

Your success depends on scrupulous adherence to peaceful means. The other side is ready to commit a hundred acts of violence if you commit one.

By the end of 1943, a pall of gloom had begun to settle on the nationalist agitation. The Freedom Brigade had been disbanded. Fifty thousand people languished in jails in different parts of the country. Every week the roster of fresh arrests grew larger. Slowly the police cordon was tightening around the few leaders who remained at large.

Jai Prakash Narayan was advised by his associates to leave the country for a while, or else to lie low somewhere until the police had given up the search, or at least until a fresh agitation preoccupied the attention of the Government. But although his health was poor and the damp weather had started, Jai Prakash Narayan's relentless travelling continued without let up.

The Punjab had not been a major participant in the 1942 movement, Jai Prakash decided that this was one area that needed a transfusion of nationalist feeling, and he went to Delhi enroute to Lahore in September 1944.

Somehow, the Delhi police learnt of JP's intentions and searched a number of apartments in Delhi, but he had already left Delhi by the Frontier Mail. However he was arrested in the train itself near Amritsar. When the train stopped at Mughalpura station JP was escorted off the train into a waiting police car that took him to Lahore Fort.

Jai Prakash Narayan, Ram Manohar Lohia and Prabhavati Devi

On the 14th December, 1943, Jai Prakash Narayan was declared a state prisoner, and his interrogation began. The Government did not want it to be known that Jai Prakash Narayan was imprisoned at Lahore Fort.

For 16 months Jai Prakash Narayan remained at Lahore Fort. Not only was he cut off from the world outside, he did not have access to the other prisoners in the fort. It took him some time to realise that Dr. Ram Manohar Lohia too was detained in the same compound.

And then in 1945 Jai Prakash and Lohia were shifted to Agra jail on an indefinite sentence. The chief of a British

Parliamentary delegation met Jai Prakash and Lohia in Agra jail.

Soon after rumours began to spread that Jai Prakash Narayan would be pardoned and released, though this was clearly not possible until the British Cabinet Mission came to India. It was also said that Mahatma Gandhi had demanded Jai Prakash's release as a proof of the sincerity of the British Government.

The Home member of the Indian Government met Jai Prakash in Agra jail. After a long discussion, Jai Prakash was asked whether he would resort to violence to win Independence. He answered, "We want independence—if we can achieve that through ahimsa, then that will be good. But if necessary, we will not shrink from using violence to attain our ends".

❑❑❑

Released from Jail

The only true antidote to the perversions of politics is more politics and better politics. Not negation of politics.

On the 11th April 1946, the whole country was electrified at the news that Jai Prakash Narayan and Dr. Lohia had been released from Agra jail. The two men were given a tumultuous welcome. From Agra, Jai Prakash Narayan went to Delhi, where he met and conferred with members of the British cabinet mission, From Delhi he was due to go to Patna, but the huge welcome which residents of that city had planned for Jai Prakash Narayan was not yet ready, and it was contrived to delay Jai Prakash Narayan at Benares to allow a few more days for the preperations.

When Jai Prakash Narayan finally arrived at Patna, he was overwhelmed by the massive crowds, the festooned streets and cries of "Jai Prakash Narayan zindabad", "Inquilab zindabad", "August Kranti Zindabad". Ramdhari Singh Dinakar read out a poem to the assembled people, and Jai Prakash Narayan was pressed to make a speech.

He said, "During the August Revolt, the Indian sepoys at Jamshedpur went on strike in sympathy with our cause, and the Government had to call in English reserves. The Congress leaders point to realise the extent of our success. Nearly 40,000 men laid down their lives in this revolution, and we are chastised for not adopting non-voilence".

Meanwhile the Cabinet Mission concluded its talks with Maulana Azad, MA Jinnah, Mahatma Gandhi and the representatives of all the parties and communities. Jinnah began the negotiations with his emphatic demand for Pakistan consisting of the six 'Muslim provinces'. The alternative which the mission put before Zinnah were either to accept a small Pakistan with full sovereign status or a large Pakistan within an Indian Union and with less sovereign powers.

As the position of the League and the Congress began to harden (Jinnah was clamouring against the conception of a "mouth-eaten" Pakistan) the cabinet mission began to workout a constitution which struck a balance between a strong, United India and an Independent Pakisthan—if that was possible. The ministers were faced with the Congress–League disagreement on almost every point of detail.

Opposing Partition of India

> *Violence becomes superfluous and harmful where Lokashakti has been aroused, and in the absence of the latter violence proves to be sterile and cruel.*

On 16th May, 1946 the Cabinet Mission published its plan rejecting the division of the country into two separate and sovereign states. Yet taking onto account the fears of the communal minority by devising three seperate bodies to draw up a constitution, Britain was to transfer power to India soon after the Indian constitutent assembly had framed a constitution. Meanwhile the administration was to be carried on by an interim Government consisting of the representatives of the Indian political parties.

There could be no agreement on the composition of the interim Government, though the Congress Working Committee accepted the mission's long term plan on the 25th June, 1946. On the 7th July that year, the All India Congress committee met in Bombay to endorse the Working Committee's resolution of the 25th June, 1946. It was at this meeting that Nehru took over the Congress presidency from

Maulana Azad. On the same day the Congress Socialist attacked the cabinet mission plan, calling it a trap laid by the British imperialist, asked the Congress Committee to reject it. Nehru with the intention of defending Congress acceptance of the plan, chose to make an equally fiery and provocative speech which led to immediate misconstructions. Jinnah saw Nehru's statements as a complete repudiation of the cabinet mission plan, and condemned the Congress for its "petty fogging and hagging attitude". Immediately, he called for 16th August, 1946 as 'direct action' day and a wave of communal rioting began. 5000 people were killed in Calcutta in 48 hours of rioting. It was the begining of a tidal wave of killing that reached gigantic proportions of half a million.

Jai Prakash Narayan and the Congress Socialists were aghast at the developments. Now that there was a real chance of esatablishing a Government that was not merely a figure head, the Congress and the League were frittering away their energies in bitter conflict. Jai Prakash Narayan made it clear that he had no truck with either of the two bodies. He castigated the Congress sharply for sacrificing its revolutionary goats, and the League for stabbing the objective of complete independence in the back.

Soon, however, it became apparent that the 'working arrangement' between the Congress and CSP had outlived its utility. The CSP had served as a useful counterfoil to the forward block and the communities. The relationship had now worn threadbare and this was becoming painfully obvious to the Socialists. ❑❑❑

Differences with Congress

You will tell me that this endless insistence on peaceful means is our Gandhian fad. But let me tell you that no such thing is being foisted on you. It is the strategy of the people's struggle that dictates this line of action.

In February 1947, the Congress Socialist Party (CSP) had a session at Kanpur to weigh the consequences of the 'shift in Congress' attitude: smarting under the implications of a recent Congress resolution that 'now the members of other parties can no longer be counted as Congressites' the CSP responded dropping the 'Congress': now it was merely the 'Socialist Party'.

On February 20, 1947 the British Labour Government announced its plan that power would be transferred to indians by a date not later than June 1948. Lord Wavell, the Viceroy returned to England and the last of British Governers-General in India, Lord Mountbatten arrived in India with a definite mission: to wind up the 182 year old British Indian Empire in 15 months.

Mountbatten spent his first few weeks in the country meeting the Indian leaders individually. The first interview with Nehru was rewarding, and mutual confidence and friendship were established between them. On the thorny question of a United India versus Pakistan the decision was made for the latter. The Congress High Command—specifically Nehru and Patel—had reconciled themselves to partition in some form by the end of 1946. Now that they were at the threshold of power they felt inclined to accept Pakistan rather than go back and continue the struggle for India's unity. Mahatma Gandhi fought a rear guard battle to save India from partition but the Congress did not accept his plan.

At one point knowing Jai Prakash Narayan's identical feelings about partition, Mahatma Gandhi asked Nehru to elect Jai Prakash Narayan as Congress president in June 1947. Nehru did not agree, and Dr. Rajendra Prasad became the President of the party instead.

Mahatma Gandhi bowed to the feeling against him, and urged unity. What was the CSP to do? Once again as at Tripura it declined to vote on the Issue. In later years this was a course which the Socialists were to bitterly regret. Sovereignty at midnight, the exact moment of India's independence. The midnight hour struck and celebrations started all over India. The British Raj had reached its last moment. It was a glorious event, one for which men like Jai Prakash Narayan had fought—but it also meant tragedy and bloodshed on an unparallelled scale. Bengal, Bihar and Punjab were aflame, millions lost their homes and their families. And as a bitter climax to this terrible event, Mahatma Gandhi the apostle of peace, was shot dead on the 30th January, 1948 in New Delhi.

The heart of Jai Prakash Narayan was broken at the behaviour of Congress during 1946-47. He refused the partition of India, as far back as the middle of 1946 and he was also aggrieved to note that Congress was engaged not in avoiding the partition but in getting the political power from the Britishers. Jai Prakash openly condemned the power usurping policy of Congress and stood in the front line along with Mahatma Gandhi to avoid the partition but Pakistan was the foregone conclusion of the political situation at the time. Jai Prakash was utterly dismayed at this attitude of Congress. He now decided to divorce from Congress ideology and party and forming of an independent socialist party to pursue socialist ideas in India accordingly.

In 1947 at Kanpur, Socialist Party of India was formed with a concrete programme of its own for bringing socialism in India.

Just one day before Gandhiji's assassination, Prabhavati had left his side to join Jai Prakash Narayan in Patna. Two days later she was back in Delhi, Jai Prakash Narayan stood next to her, his eyes clouded with grief and sorrow.

Those days, the constitutional foundations of a new India were being laid. For weeks, the Constituent Assembly put together the fabric of a document which would shape the destiny of a new nation. Jai Prakash Narayan however did not accept the membership of the Assembly. He felt that its members did not represent the people of India.

The party of Jai Prakash Narayan survived till 1952 General Election when the socialists suffered a setback in a crushing defeat. It was actually the policy of Congress to defeat socialist candidates in the general election. Jai Pakash cited many examples of sabotage by Congress against the socialist candidates. In 1952 itself Jai Prakash had to come out of the Socialist party formed by him because of differences and putting of all blames for the defeat in 1952 general election on his shoulders by other leaders of the party.

This shows the idealogical hollowcast of socialist thinking in India. Though Jai Prakash Narayan could not be blamed for the defeat but it can be said that Jai Prakash lacked the political patience and he went on experimenting with this or that party till the end of his life.

In 1952-53 Jai Prakash Narayan was instrumental in formation of a new party namely 'Praja Socialist Party' with the help of break away fraction of Socialist party and a small group of Socialists namely peasants and workers party in Maharashtra. But this experiment also could not materialise. Then a turning point came in Jai Prakash's political life which can be easily termed as the second phase of his political career from 1952 to 1970.

Jai Prakash Narayan was then not in active politics and engaged himself in 'Bhoodan' work of Vinoba Bhave and Sarvodaya work of 'Sarva Sewa Sangh' formed by Mahatma Gandhi. In the second phase of Jai Prakash's political life, he made an assessment of the social evils in India and tried to provide a solution to various social problems mainly through hard conversion. This period observes him mainly engaged in Sarvodaya work.

❑❑❑

As Socio-Political Activist

We in the Sarvodaya movement emphasise the initiative of the people—the Lokashakti as against the Rajashakti (the power of the State).

Jai Prakash Narayan was a strong believer in socialism but he often has disagreed with the means suggested to bring about socialism. Soviet model he totally discarded. He was strongly opposed to violent means for bringing socialism. Jai Prakash's party suffered a crushing defeat in the 1952 general elections, yet this defeat could not shake his belief in socialism. In fact the very creed of Jai Prakash is that of an activist who does not care the defeats. But Socialist party was a new party and it could not sustain the

Morarji Desai, Jai Prakash Narayan and L.K. Advani

shock of defeat and therefore Jai Prakash tried to engage party workers in Bhoodan movement of Vinobaji.

In May, 1952 at Pachmarhi conference of Socialist party, Jai Prakash himself donated half of his land in Bhoodan movement. In the meantime Jai Prakash was instrumental in uniting his Socialist party with that of Acharya Kriplani's Kissan Mazdoor Praja Party and formed a new party—Praja Socialist Party.

Vinoba's influence on Jai Prakash increased slowly. In June 1952, Jai Prakash decided for 21 day fast for purification. The fast continued from 23rd June 1952 to 13th of July 1952. This 21 days fast completely changed him from a Marxist to a Sarvodayait. He, therefore, decided to join Bhoodan movement entirely. He joined Vinobaji in Bihar and his arrival had a great impact on Bhoodan movement.

In 1953 there came an invitation from Jawahar Lal Nehru to discuss cooperation issue between Congress and Socialists. Though Jai Prakash Narayan agreed yet other socialists could not. Jai Prakash insisted upon Nehru to accept 14-point programme discussed in part but Nehru refused to do so. Though Jai Prakash-Nehru talks could yield nothing but its reprecussions on Jai Prakash's part was great and soon it was evident that the party was going to split. Jai Prakash resigned from the secretaryship of the party.

Jai Prakash soon lost the interest in active politics. He was inclined to get more and more involved in Bhoodan work. He decided to give his whole life for the Bhoodan movement. This pleadge of his to devote whole life for Bhoodan movement is known as 'Jeevan dan pledge'.

Jai Prakash Narayan had other motive in mind. He wanted to live the life of a sage. Though retired from active politics his socialist friends all comes the world. He attended Asian Socialist Conference in Bombay in 1956.

In 1958, he toured Europe on an invitation from the European socialist friends. During his 18-week tour of Europe he preached Sarvodaya which, according to him, was a Gandhian way of socialism.

Jai Prakash now finally decided to cut all connections with political parties, including his own party of which he was still a member. He, therefore, wanted to resign but was advised contararily by his friends. But in 1957 Jai Prakash sent a long letter of resignation to Praja Socialist Party.

Though Jai Prakash was disinterested in active politics but he could never have been a dumb spectator to the international happenings when Russia sent its army in Hungary to crush a Rebellian there in 1956, he strongly condemned the action and called it a communist imperialist action. In 1959, when China annexed Tibet forcefully Jai Prakash was vociferous in condemning this action.

On the national scenario Jai Prakash condemned action of the Indian Army in Goa in 1961. He wanted the relaease of Sheikh Abdullah without trial for which he was trying since 1953. He also wanted good relations with Pakistan and became the president of Indo-Pak concialitory group in 1962.

Jai Prakash Narayan was also instrumental in supporting the armed struggle in Nepal during 1953-55. He further criticized Chinese agression on India in 1962 and in 1963 he, alongwith another sarvodayait Shanker Rao Deo, organized a long peace march from Delhi to Peking. However, due to refusal of Chinese Government to permit the march in the Chinese territory, it ended at Gauhati in Assam.

JP organized relief works on a large scale during Bihar famine in 1966. A commitee was formed in October 1966. JP succeeded in getting the cooperation of not only the Bihar and the Central Government, but also of various organisations such as Bharat Sevak Samaj, Bihar Sarvodaya Mandal, Bihar Khadi-Gramodyoga Sangh, Indian Women's Council, Bihar Chamber of Commerce and all the political parties in Bihar. There was a resounding response to his appeal for funds from various cities such as Calcutta and Bombay. While touring the famine-stricken districts of Bihar, he, however, warned the Bihari people that Bihar must not become a state of beggars or parasites. He exhorted Bihari Kisans to face the natual calamity with determination and to double their efforts to grow more food as soon as conditions became normal.

Jai Prakash Narayan was keenly observing the events in east Pakistan (Now Bangladesh) during 1970-71 and was disturbed at the atrocities of the Pakistan Army over Bengali

Muslims in East Pakistan. He was also disturbed over the ever increasing influx of refugees in India due to genocide of Bangali Muslims by Pak army in East Pakistan. He toured over 16 countries to put forward the cause of Bangladesh and the refugees as government of India spokesman.

Jai Prakash Narayan was instrumental in solving the Dacoit Problem in the Chambal Valley in 1971-72.

The dacoit chiefs, including the dreaded Moharsingh and Madhosingh, were ready to surrender arms and themselves along with their gangmates only before Jai Prakash Narayan. So functions were organised first at Gandhi Ashram, Jaora in Morena district and later at Chhatarpur in Bundelkhand, at Gwa-lior and Bhopal, where not less than 450 dacoits in all laid down their arms ceremoniously. Both Jai Prakashji and Shri P.C. Sethi, then Chief Minister of Madhya Pradesh, were present at almost all the functions.

It was indeed a social miracle which had its origin in the surrender of about 20 dacoits in 1960 before Vinobaji. Nothing that Jai Prakash Narayan had done during the previous two decades had brought him such spontaneous and immense acclamation as did the surrender of Chambal and the Bundelkhand dacoits at his instance in 1972.

Emergency and Final Days

Non-materialism, by rejecting matter as the ultimate reality immediately elevates the individual to a moral plane and urges him to endeavour to realize his own true nature and fulfill the purpose of his being.

Though Jai Prakash Narayan had decided long back not to enter active politics, yet he could not fail to observe the plight of the Indian people during the eighties. After the Bangladesh crisis was over the then Prime Minister Mrs. Indira Gandhi ordered midterm elections to Lok Sabha in 1971. Congress(I) won

Postal Stamp on Jai Prakash Narayan

with thumping majority in Lok Sabha but the problems of the people remained.

JP keenly observed the onslaught of majority over democracy through Mrs. Gandhi's actions corruption, arrogancy, atrocities, and other evils were the order of the day.

In Gujarat the students demanded end to corruption, solution unemployment problem and various other demands and through a long agitation succeded in getting the Gujarat assembly dissolved. Before that Jai Prakash had published an Article "Youth for Democracy" which had enthused the students of Gujarat. The students of Bihar also decided to conduct similar struggle on the Gujarat lines and requested Jai Prakash Narayan to lead their struggle.

By that time, Jai Prakash Narayan was not satisfactorily over the Sarvodaya Progress and had come to the conclusion that Sarvodaya can not solve the immense socio-economic problems of the Indian masses. He was also dissatisfied that Vinobaji had discarded Satyagraha as a useful weapon. He therefore decided to lead the students agitation in Bihar. He was deeply grieved over the brutal atrocities of police and other para-military forces on the peaceful yet determined agitators, and gave a clarion call for a total revolution.

This movement succeeded in reaching the grass root levels in Bihar in 1974-75 and spread almost in every nook and corner of the country. JP became leader of masses and the people looked to him as their sole saviour.

Mrs. Indira Gandhi had other motives in her mind and was adamant in accepting the 13-point charter of the Bihar students which included among other things dissolution of the Bihar Assembly and dismissal of the Bihar Ministry. She tried to suppress the movement, and failing to do so, ultimately declared national emergency under article 352 of Constitution of India on 25th June, 1975. Before that the Allahabad high court had declared her election invlid on the grounds of malpractices in elections. This she took as a challange by the devisive and reactionary forces.

The events between 26th June 1975 to 18th March 1977 are well known to the nation when almost all the opposition leaders were arrested and sent to jail. Jai Prakash Narayan himself was put under imprisonment at Chandigarh, there he felt remarkably ill yet the Congress government was determined to have a show down with him.

In March 1977 the mid-term elections were ordered and Mrs. Indira Gandhi was defeated. A new party, namely Janta Party, came into power. This party was combination of major political parties that participated in Bihar agitation. But this party also could not give answer to people' problems. Though Jai Prakash Narayan had high hopes yet his dream of total revolution could not be materialised in his life time. Disillusiond and disheartend Jai Prakash Narayan passed away on 8th October, 1979 at Patna in Bihar.

Jai Prakash Narayan was known as Lok Nayak (People's Hero) for his credible work in the field of social reforms and independent activism for Sampoorna Kranti (Total Revolution). He was posthumously awarded India's greatest civilian award, the Bharat Ratna in 1999. He was also awarded the Magsaysay Award on account of his excellent public service. ❏❏❏

Timeline

- **1902** : Born on 11th October at Sitab-diara village of Bihar

- **1920** : Married to Prabhavati Devi

- **1922** : Went to US for higher studies

- **1929** : Returned to India and joined the Indian National Congress on the Invitation of Jawaharlal Nehru

- **1932** : Arrested and imprisoned in Nasik Jail, where he met Ram Manohar Lohia and other national leaders

- **1934** : Dedicated his life to the struggle for freedom

- **1934** : Became the Secretary of the Socialist Party

- **1939** : Arrested for opposing Indian Participation in World War II

- **1942** : Participated in Quit India Movement, arrested and escaped from jail

- **1943** : Raised Freedom Brigade, Arrested again

- **1946** : Finally released from prison

- **1947** : India gained independence on 15th August

- **1948** : Left the Congress Party

- **1952** : Formed the Praja Socialist Party

- **1957** : Officially split with the Praja Socialist Party in order to pursue Public Service

- **1965** : Awarded Magsaysay award for Public Service

- **1950-74** : Remained with Acharya Vinoba Bhave and took an active part in Bhoodan and Sarvodya Movement

- **1972** : Visited Chambal Valley and persuaded several dreaded acoits to surrender

- **1974** : Participated in the Gujarat Nav Nirman Andolan

- **1974** : Stood against the corrupt and increasingly undemocratic government of then Prime Minister Indira Gandhi

- **1974** : On the 5th of June called for Sampurna Kranti–Total Revolution at a historic rally of students at Patna's Gandhi Maidan

- **1975** : Arrested and kept in prison during 'Emergency'

- **1979** : On October 8th, passed away at Patna, Bihar

- **1999** : Awarded the Bharat Ratna

❏ ❏ ❏